BRITISH HISTORY

The Middle Ages

1154–1485

KINGFISHER

KINGFISHER
Kingfisher Publications Plc
New Penderel House, 283–288 High Holborn
London WC1V 7HZ
www.kingfisherpub.com

Material in this edition previously published by Kingfisher Publications Plc
in *Children's Illustrated Encyclopedia of British History* in 1992

This revised, reformatted and updated edition published by
Kingfisher Publications Plc in 2002

1TR/0202/PROSP/RNB/140MA

2 4 6 8 10 9 7 5 3 1

A CIP catalogue record for this book is available from the British Library

ISBN 0 7534 0099 5

Printed in China

Consultant: David Haycock
Editor: James Harrison,
with Jean Coppendale and Honor Head
Designer: Edward Kinsey
Proofreader: Frances Clapham
Indexer: Isobel McLean
Cover design: Mike Davis

CONTENTS

THE PLANTAGENETS
(1154 – 1399)

T HE PLANTAGENETS RULED ENGLAND for almost 250 years. These were years of strife and violence, but they also saw the beginnings of English democracy in the birth of Parliament. It was Plantagenet kings who fought the Hundred Years War against the French, initially winning most of the battles but losing the war and most of England's French possessions. The name Plantagenet was a nickname for the founder of the dynasty, Geoffrey of Anjou, who wore a sprig of broom, *planta genista*, as a badge. But the name does not appear to have been used by the royal family itself until the mid-1400s so some historians prefer to call Henry II and his sons Angevins, men from Anjou.

Geoffrey Plantagenet, Count of Anjou, whose son began 250 years of Plantagenet rule in Britain.

Henry II

Henry OF ANJOU, the son of Matilda and Geoffrey of Anjou, became Henry II, the first Plantagenet King of England, in 1154. He immediately set about ruthlessly destroying the castles of those barons who had opposed him during Stephen's reign. He also wanted more control over the Church, which had a powerful hold over ordinary people during these times.

THOMAS à BECKET

In 1155 Henry appointed his friend, a priest Thomas à Becket, as Chancellor, the chief minister of England. Later, in 1162, Henry persuaded Becket to become Archbishop of Canterbury. He thought that as both Archbishop and Chancellor Becket would do his bidding and help keep the Church in check. But Becket "put God before the king" and defended the rights and possessions of the Church. Henry set out his Church reforms in the Constitutions of Clarendon in 1164 – including the trial of clergy in the Crown's courts, not the Church's own courts. Becket and Henry were in such bitter conflict that twice Becket had to flee to France. When he returned the second time in 1170, Henry is said to have cried out in anger: "Who will rid me of this turbulent priest?" Four knights took Henry at his word, went to Canterbury and brutally murdered Becket at the foot of the altar steps in the cathedral. This aroused horror in Europe and Becket was made a saint.

Above: **Henry II (1154-1189) was one of the most powerful rulers of the Middle Ages. A man of great humour but violent temper, he brought England a time of peace and prosperity.**

TIME CHART

● **1154** Henry II King of England (to 1189). Henry appoints Thomas à Becket Lord Chancellor

● **1162** Thomas à Becket appointed Archbishop of Canterbury. Henry raises Danegeld for the last time

● **1163** Oxford University established

● **1164** Constitutions of Clarendon: clerics condemned by the Church to be punished by lay courts. Becket goes into exile

● **1170** Henry has his son crowned king to ensure succession. Becket is murdered in Canterbury Cathedral

● **1171** Henry invades Ireland and the Irish princes submit

● **1172** Synod of Cashel: Irish Church reformed along English lines. Henry absolved of murder of Becket

● **1173** Henry's family rebel in France. Barons in England join them. Henry crushes revolt in France and imprisons Queen Eleanor. Becket made a saint

Left: On December 29, 1170, Thomas à Becket was murdered on the steps of the altar of Canterbury Cathedral for having opposed the king. Many miracles were soon reported at his tomb. He was made a saint three years later.

Below: **In 1173 Henry II ruled more of France than the French king, Louis VII.**

THE INVASION OF IRELAND

England's long and troubled involvement in Ireland began in the reign of Henry II. Henry took advantage of the fact that Irish clan chiefs were fighting each other to claim the title of *Ard-Rí*, or High King. In 1166 he sent a force led by Richard de Clare, Earl of Pembroke, who was also known as Strongbow, to support the King of Leinster in Ireland. In 1171 Strongbow invaded Ireland, claiming the authority of the Pope to convert the Irish Celtic Church to the Roman Church. Irish kings, nobles and bishops submitted to his forces in the same year.

HENRY II'S SONS

Henry II had four strong-willed and unruly sons: Henry, Richard, Geoffrey and John. Henry, the eldest, was known as the Young King because his father had him crowned during his own lifetime to protect the succession. Henry II gave each of his three elder sons lands from his French possessions: the Young King had Normandy, Maine and Anjou; Richard had Aquitaine; Geoffrey had Brittany; but John received no territories to rule and so people at the time nicknamed him Lackland.

The four sons were encouraged by their mother Eleanor, to rebel against the king. She had already fallen out with Henry II in an unhappy marriage. Henry and Geoffrey both died before their father. Henry II fought against Richard and John and kept Eleanor imprisoned for much of their married life. Henry's sons never succeeded in overthrowing him.

THE CRUSADES

Since the Norman times Anglo-Norman knights had become involved in the crusades. The crusades were a series of military expeditions undertaken by European Christians over 3,000 kilometres away in the Middle East. Their aim was to recover the Holy Lands, where Christianity began, from Muslim occupation. There were eight major crusades from 1095 to 1270, most of which were failures, though a Christian kingdom of Jerusalem was briefly established. During the Middle Ages, many men and women made journeys, called pilgrimages, to Jerusalem and other holy places in Palestine where Jesus had lived and died.

Left: **The Archbishop of Canterbury is the head of the Church of England. The first archbishop was St Augustine, who founded an abbey in Canterbury in 597. Archbishop Lanfranc laid the foundations for the Cathedral from 1070-1089. Thomas à Becket was murdered in the cathedral in 1170 and his tomb there became a centre of pilgrimage.**

FOCUS ON A MEDIEVAL MARKET

Most medieval towns had fairs and markets. Markets were usually held once a week, when farmers from local villages would bring their produce and livestock to sell. There were stalls for butter, salt and fish, as well as shops selling pies for a penny. Metal, leather and woodwork would also be for sale. Beggars and pick-pockets mingled with the crowds looking at the many craft and food stalls while jugglers, musicians and dancing bears entertained passers-by.

This picture shows a stone cross from the late 14th century in the market square at Chichester in West Sussex. Official business would be done in the market hall at the centre of the square. Many such halls survive today, for example, in Chipping Campden in Gloucestershire and Chipping Norton in Oxfordshire (chipping means selling). Some larger medieval towns had annual fairs where merchants and traders from other parts of the country and overseas exchanged goods. St Giles Fair, held in Oxford, dates back to medieval times.

Richard I and the Crusades

THE CHRISTIAN CHURCH had lost control of the Holy Lands to the Arabs in the 7th century. The Arabs were Muslims and followed Mohammed, founder of the religion of Islam. At first they let Christian pilgrims visit the holy places. But when Muslim Turks invaded the region they began to attack the Christian pilgrims.

In 1095 Pope Urban II called on Christians to liberate Jerusalem from the Turks. Up to 25,000 people, from knights to paupers, travelled to Constantinople, and went on to capture Jerusalem in 1099 in the First Crusade.

Above: **A knight of the crusades.**

A famous legend tells of Blondel, a minstrel who tirelessly searched for, and found, the lost king. Richard was rescued only when his long-suffering subjects paid an enormous ransom - but they warmly welcomed him back to London. Soon, however, he left for Normandy to defend his French lands. Richard was mortally wounded by an archer while

Right: **Saladin, the great Muslim general and sultan of the Saracens. He united the Muslim kingdoms and from 1187 led them in a *jihad* (holy war) against the Christian crusaders – among them Richard the Lionheart, King of England.**

THE THIRD CRUSADE

Nearly 100 years later English knights were among the main participants in the Third Crusade. The great Muslim leader, Saladin had recaptured Jerusalem from the crusaders in 1187. Richard I came to the throne in 1189 as a soldier already admired for his skill and courage. His bravery earned him the name *Coeur de Lion*, the Lionheart.

That year Richard responded to the Pope's call to try to win Jerusalem back from the Muslim Turks. He came within sight of Jerusalem, but never recaptured it from the Muslims. He did, however, secure a five-year peace treaty with Saladin. This allowed European pilgrims to visit the holy places again. During negotiations, Saladin sent Richard, who had become ill, fresh fruit and snow water to help him recover.

RICHARD: THE ABSENT KING

On his way home from the Holy Lands, Richard was captured, handed over to his enemy, the Holy Roman Emperor Henry VI, and held prisoner.

Left: **Richard I, (on the right) wearing the red cross of the crusaders. He led an army of knights to the Holy Land in 1189 on the Third Crusade.**

besieging the castle of Chaluz, in France, in 1199. Richard spent only seven months of his ten-year reign in Britain – and that was to raise money for the Third Crusade by selling Church and state lands and charters of self-government to the towns.

IMPACT OF THE CRUSADES

The crusades may have been a military failure for Europe, but returning crusaders brought back with them valuable spices, such as nutmeg and cinnamon, along with sugar, cotton and Oriental tapestries. They also brought back Arabic ideas about science, medicine, philosophy and art.

Below: **A battle between Muslims and Christian knights. The crusaders sewed big crosses onto their clothes, having taken up the call of the Pope to "wear Christ's cross as your badge. If you are killed your sins will be pardoned". Some knights who were also monks formed a full-time regiment in Jerusalem called the Knights of St John, or the Knights Hospitallers.**

- **1174** Henry II does penance at Canterbury for Becket's murder. William of Scotland invades Northumberland and is captured. Henry crushes English revolt and makes peace with his sons. Treaty of Falaise: William of Scotland freed after paying homage to Henry

- **1176** Assize of Northampton: Henry establishes judicial rules. Eisteddfod held at Cardigan

- **1178** Henry establishes Central Court of Justice

- **1179** Grand Assize of Windsor curbs power of feudal courts

- **1180** Wells Cathedral begun

- **1186** Henry makes peace with Philip II of France

- **1187** Henry and Philip of France agree to go on the Third Crusade

- **1188** Richard, third son of Henry, does homage to Philip II

- **1189** Philip and Richard force Henry to acknowledge Richard as heir. Death of Henry: Richard I succeeds him (to 1199). Massacre of Jews at Richard's coronation

- **1189-1192** Richard and Philip of France lead Third Crusade but fail to take Jerusalem

- **1191** Civil war in England between Richard's brother John and William Longchamp

- **1192** Leopold of Austria captures Richard as he travels to England

- **1193** John claims the throne

- **1194** Richard is freed and returns to England; John flees to France

- **1199** Richard killed at siege of Chaluz; John succeeds him (to 1216)

The Magna Carta

KING JOHN, RICHARD'S BROTHER, was a tough, energetic man. Like many other Plantagenets, he was given to violent rages and cruelty. One of his early acts as king was to order the murder of his nephew, Arthur, whom he had imprisoned at Rouen in France. This young prince, as son of John's older brother Geoffrey, had a good claim to the throne.

Arthur's murder and John's behaviour provoked the barons of Anjou and Poitou into fighting against John. He lost most of his French lands and also angered the Pope by refusing to accept his choice of Archbishop of Canterbury. When John took the clergy's lands, Pope Innocent III banned nearly all Church services in England.

KING JOHN AGAINST THE BARONS

John continued to confiscate Church property, so in 1213 the Pope declared that John was no longer the rightful king of England, and granted Philip of France the right to depose him. As John had already angered his English barons by taxing them harshly and abusing feudal rights, it was not long before the English barons joined forces and rebelled against the king.

In June 1215 John was forced to meet the barons in a meadow beside the River Thames at Runnymede. There John put his seal to a document the barons had drawn up to confirm their rights against the king. This document was the famous Magna Carta, or Great Charter. It established certain curbs on royal abuses of power and laid the foundation for British democracy.

Above: **The Children's Crusade in 1212 involved possibly up to 50,000 French and German children who tried to reach the Holy Land. Most were turned back or were sold as slaves.**

- **1201** John grants a charter to Jews

- **1203** Arthur of Brittany, John's nephew, murdered

- **1204** Philip of France conquers Normandy from John

- **1205** Dispute over new Archbishop of Canterbury: John nominates John de Grey, Bishop of Norwich

- **1206** Pope Innocent III rejects de Grey's nomination, supports election of Stephen Langton as Archbishop of Canterbury

- **1207** John rejects Langton. Port of Liverpool founded

- **1208** Pope puts England under interdict, or exclusion. Llewelyn the Great seizes Powys

Below: **The English succession. Claimants to the Crown are underlined.**

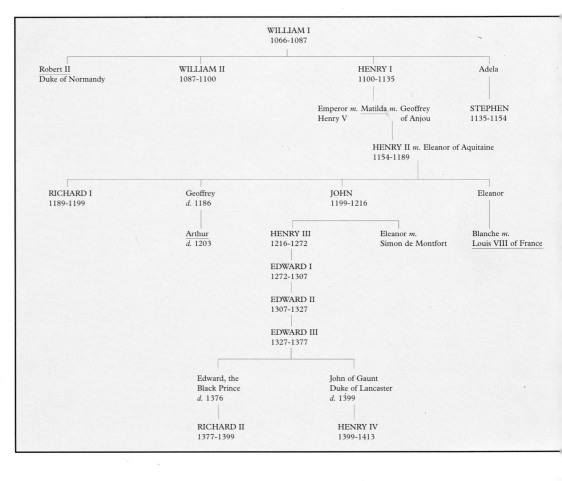

WHAT THE CHARTER SET OUT

Four original copies of the Magna Carta exist, one each in Lincoln and Salisbury Cathedrals and two in the British Museum. Most of the 63 clauses in the Magna Carta pledged the king to upholding the feudal system of the barons, but some also protected the rights of freemen, those citizens not tied to feudal lords. Clauses which have had great influence included the following: in all important matters the king must seek the barons' advice; no special taxes could be raised without the barons' consent; no freeman (those not tied to feudal lords) should be imprisoned or exiled, or deprived of property, except by the law of the land; and (one of the most important clauses) "to none will we sell, to none will we deny or delay right of justice". This ensured the basic right of free justice for all regardless of the seriousness of the crime or the individual's wealth or position.

After all the trouble with Rome, the Church was to be formally guaranteed certain long sought-after rights including freedom from state control, and the right to elect archbishops, bishops, abbots and other senior Church representatives.

EFFECT OF THE CHARTER

The effect of the Charter was that the king could continue to rule, but must keep to the laws of the land, and could be forced to do so. The Magna Carta was in force for only a few weeks before John persuaded the Pope to revoke it. Civil war broke out and John died in 1216. The Magna Carta was reissued in a revised form and, in 1225, became the law of the land.

Above: **King John's great seal which was attached to the Magna Carta. It showed the King's agreement so turning the Charter into law.**

Right: **A page from the Magna Carta. There are four copies of the Magna Carta: one each in Lincoln and Salisbury Cathedrals, and two in the British Museum.**

- **1209** London Bridge completed (stands until 1832). Some scholars leave Oxford for Cambridge (the beginning of Cambridge University)

- **1213** Philip II of France accepts Pope's mandate to conquer England. John accepts Langton as Archbishop of Canterbury; papal interdict is lifted. English ships destroy French fleet

- **1214** French defeat English and allies at battle of Bouvines. Barons threaten revolt. John takes crusader vows, and in return Pope excommunicates the barons

- **1215** John agrees to Magna Carta. Pope annuls Magna Carta; civil war resumes

- **1216** Louis of France invades England. John dies: succeeded by son Henry III, aged 9 (to 1272). William Marshal becomes regent. Magna Carta reissued

- **1217** William Marshal defeats the French at the battle of Lincoln; French leave England

Rivals for the Throne

Henry III came to the throne aged only nine as John's eldest son. In his youth the country was well governed for him by William Marshal, Earl of Pembroke, and then by Hubert de Burgh, who was the Justiciar. When he grew up Henry III came under the influence of foreign barons and courtiers: first Peter des Roches from Poitou, Bishop of Winchester, and then des Roches' nephew (or perhaps son), Peter des Rivaux. Henry married Eleanor of Provence in 1236, and her many uncles from Savoy were given large estates and positions of power. Chief among them was Peter of Savoy, to whom Henry gave an estate near London, by the Thames; the Savoy Hotel and Theatre now stand on this site.

Although Henry III was a pious, sensitive man, he was completely without any ability to govern by himself. His inept and spendthrift ways upset the English nobles (those original Norman barons who came to England during the Norman Conquest).

SIMON DE MONTFORT

One of these nobles was Simon de Montfort, who came to England in 1229 to claim the earldom of Leicester, which he inherited through his grandmother. De Montfort quickly became a favourite of Henry, and of the king's sister Eleanor, whom he married. Henry's misrule and his reliance on foreigners made the barons take up arms against him. They assembled a Great Council in Oxford in 1258, and with de Montfort as their leader they forced the king to swear to the Provisions of Oxford, in return for financial help to cover his debts. These Provisions said that the king was to rule with the advice of a council of barons.

WELSH RESISTANCE

The conquest of Wales was carried out by powerful barons known as the Lords Marchers, because they guarded the marches, or frontiers, between Wales and England. The wild northern regions of Wales remained largely independent and it was in North Wales at this time that the Welsh archers developed the longbow, which became one of the most formidable weapons of its day.

Above: Henry III (1216-1272) became king at the age of nine but did not rule until 1234. Simon de Montfort and the English barons rebelled against his favouritism and promotion of foreign men at Court.

Below: English bases in North Wales. Massive castles were built at key sites to control the Welsh.

Above: Simon de Montfort, leader of the dissatisfied barons, as shown in a window of Chartres Cathedral.

Below: Caernarfon Castle was built as a royal residence. The Eagle Tower is about 22 metres in diameter. The central gate had five double doors.

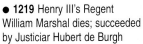

● **1219** Henry III's Regent William Marshal dies; succeeded by Justiciar Hubert de Burgh

● **1224** The king recovers royal castles held by the barons. Louis VIII of France declares war

● **1225** Henry reissues Magna Carta and Charter of the Forests, in return for grant of general tax

● **1227** Henry declares himself to be of age to rule; but Hubert de Burgh retains power

● **1228** Death of Stephen Langton. Llewelyn the Great besieges Montgomery; Henry relieves city. Sixth Crusade: Jerusalem taken

● **1229** Llewelyn nominates his son David as his successor. Henry tries to take an army to France to recover his lands, but de Burgh fails to provide shipping

● **1230** Henry's French campaign fails

● **1231** England and France make a truce

● **1232** Henry dismisses de Burgh. Peter des Roches, Bishop of Winchester, becomes adviser to the king

Above: Two knights fight each other in a mock battle, or joust, at a tournament. Each knight had his coat-of-arms on his shield, on the crest of his helmet and on his horse's trappings.

LLEWELYN THE GREAT

One of the leading princes of Wales in the early 13th century was Llewelyn the Great, prince of Gwynedd in North Wales. Llewelyn was also accepted as leader by the people of South Wales. In the early part of the reign of Henry III, Llewelyn was driven back from South Wales by the Regent, William Marshal, Earl of Pembroke. But Llewelyn increased his territory to include Gwynedd, Clwyd, Powys and part of Dyfed. His younger son, David, became Prince of Gwynedd from 1240 to 1246.

Below: Longbow archers prepare to fire their arrows. A good archer could shoot ten arrows a minute accurately over a distance of 180 metres.

LLEWELYN THE LAST

In 1246 the throne passed to David's nephews Llewelyn ap Gruffydd (the Last) and his brother Owen. Threatened by claims on Wales from Henry III and others, the brothers united and fought with such determination that, by the Peace of Woodstock in 1247, Henry was forced to recognize them as rightful rulers, so long as they paid homage to him. Llewelyn later declared himself Prince of Wales, up to that time the English had only known him as Lord of Snowdon. In 1282 he died in a rebellion against Edward I and earned the title Llewelyn the Last.

DE MONTFORT RULES ENGLAND

In 1261 Henry persuaded the Pope to absolve him from his oath under the Provisions of Oxford, and won over many barons who now disliked de Montfort's high-handed ways. De Montfort, who had gone abroad, returned to lead a rebellion which restored the Provisions of Oxford. Louis IX of France was then asked to act as judge, and decided in Henry's favour. At this, de Montfort resorted to arms, and in 1264 defeated and captured Henry III at the battle of Lewes, on the Sussex Downs. De Montfort ruled England in the king's name and summoned a parliament which gave the barons greater control over the king.

THE BEGINNINGS OF PARLIAMENT

The term parliament comes from the French word *parleyment*, or talking place. Parliament as a royal council of the English kings came into existence during the reign of Henry III. But the idea of a king's council went back to the Anglo-Saxon Witan, and later the *Curia Regis*, or King's Council, of the Norman king, Henry I. The king usually only called the council when he wanted loans or advice. It was made up of bishops and nobles who held land granted to them by the king.

Simon de Montfort's Parliament was different because when he called an assembly (with the king still as prisoner) in 1265 he did not invite just the barons. He also summoned the elected representatives of the counties, called knights of the shire, and two burgesses from each city or large town. For the first time ever, all classes of people were included, except villeins and serfs.

Left: Edward I (1272-1307) was nicknamed "Longshanks" because he was very tall and had long arms and legs. He was a skilful general and a strong and respected leader. He was also devoted to his queen, Eleanor.

This was to become the beginning of a separate council from the king's council of lords – the House of Commons. The first Act of Parliament to be recorded was the Statute of Merton in 1275. It allowed landlords to enclose common land and also declared that children born out of marriage were considered illegitimate.

While Parliament was meeting, some barons quarrelled with de Monfort, and Henry I's son, Edward, defeated and killed de Montfort at the battle of Evesham in 1265. During his lifetime de Montfort was so popular with the English people that he was known as Good Sir Simon. Henry III took control of the kingdom again until his death in 1272.

EDWARD I: THE LAWGIVER

Edward I, who was 33 when he came to the throne in 1272, was brisk, capable, and an experienced general. His love of order led him to reform the government.

The many laws passed in Edward's reign have earned him the nickname of the Lawgiver. He was the first English king to use Parliament as an instrument of government to reform the law of the land. Among his early reforms were three Statutes of Westminster, all of which dealt with local government and the ownership and inheritance of land. The Statute of Wales marked the end of Wales as a separate country; but left Welsh common law, language and customs intact. Edward also built impressive castles in North Wales from 1283 to 1307, including Caernarfon which is still standing today.

Below: **The Middle Ages, or medieval period as it is also known, was a time of wars across the borders in Scotland and Wales, and violence in England with barons struggling against the king and against each other. Castles were built and walled towns had to be well guarded with soldiers on sentry duty day and night.**

- **1233** Revolt of Richard Marshal, Earl of Pembroke, allied with Llewelyn. Richard defeats royal forces near Monmouth

- **1234** Henry III makes peace with Richard. Richard murdered in Ireland

- **1237** Barons insist on nominating three of Henry's counsellors

- **1240** Llewelyn the Great dies; succeeded by son David (to 1246)

- **1241** Henry leads expedition to Wales. Peter of Savoy, uncle of Queen Eleanor is royal adviser

- **1242** Henry defeated by Louis IX of France. Barons refuse to pay for French war

- **1245** Building of Westminster Abbey is begun

- **1246** Welsh prince David dies; succeeded by Llewelyn the Last (to 1282) and his brother Owen

- **1257** Llewelyn assumes the title Prince of Wales

- **1258** Provisions of Oxford: barons take control of Henry's government

- **1261** Pope absolves Henry from the oath to observe the Provisions of Oxford

- **1262** Llewelyn attacks England

- **1263** Simon de Montfort returns as leader of the barons; Henry accepts the barons' terms

- **1264** Battle of Lewes: de Montfort defeats and captures Henry

- **1265** De Montfort's Parliament. Battle of Evesham: Henry's son Edward defeats and kills de Montfort

- **1266** Roger Bacon invents the magnifying glass

- **1267** Henry recognizes Llewelyn as Prince of Wales

WAR WITH SCOTLAND

In Scotland, the barons asked Edward to choose a successor to Alexander III, Edward's brother-in-law, who had died without an heir in 1286. Edward I selected John Balliol as ruler of Scotland but treated him as a puppet king. The barons rebelled and in 1296 Edward invaded Scotland and captured Balliol. For ten years after this Scotland was without a king. Edward tried to rule it himself, but he was defied by William Wallace, who led an uprising and made himself master of Scotland. Wallace was an extraordinary general who managed to inspire half-armed peasant foot soldiers to take on the might of mail-clad knights. However, Edward reconquered the country and captured Wallace, who was put to death in 1305.

ROBERT BRUCE AND BANNOCKBURN

Within months of William Wallace's death, Robert Bruce became the great champion of Scotland. He was crowned King of Scotland at Scone in 1306, but an English army was quickly on the scene and Bruce suffered two heavy defeats. After a spell in hiding, Bruce defeated an English army twice as strong as his own at the battle of Bannockburn in 1314. This battle ensured that Scotland would stay independent of England.

In 1320 at the abbey of Arbroath, in Angus, an assembly of Scottish lords drew up a declaration of independence. It affirmed loyalty to Robert Bruce. Edward II agreed to a truce with Scotland. First the Treaty of Northampton brought peace to the two countries of England and Scotland. Then the Treaty of Brigham conceded to the Scots that the laws of Scotland were to be respected as independent of those of England. It also confirmed that Scotland itself was to be independent of England, with a distinct border, and that no Scottish subject could be forced to attend an English court.

EDWARD II

The first Prince of Wales became King Edward II in 1307. He was the fourth son of Edward I but his older brothers had all died when he was a boy. Edward therefore relied very much on his friends and favourites, and they in turn influenced his decisions in matters of state, to the fury of the barons. Edward's favourites included Piers Gaveston, whom a group of lords seized and beheaded in 1312. Later, Edward became fiercely loyal to Hugh Despenser and his son, also named Hugh. When the younger Hugh married Edward's cousin, the barons rebelled.

EDWARD III

Edward was only 14 years old when he came to the throne of England. His mother, Isabella of France, and her lover, Roger Mortimer, Earl of March, had ordered Edward II's murder in 1327, and had secured Edward III's succession with Parliament's support. For three years real power lay with this couple. But in 1330 Edward III rebelled against them and took charge of the government.

Right: **Springtime sowing in the countryside in the mid-1300s. Although this was a period marked by royal murders and fighting between barons, as well as war in France, ordinary people got on with their lives. All but 10 percent of the population lived and worked on the land. The earth was ploughed in rough strips from March onwards. The sower scattered the seeds by hand in the furrows of the ploughed ground, not stopping to cover it. Bird scarers used slings and other distractions to stop birds from taking the seeds. The summer months were for haymaking, and the corn was harvested in early September. From 1350 the Black Death was to cut the work force by more than one third.**

Above: **The battle of Bannockburn in 1314 was a humiliating defeat for the English and a triumph for Robert Bruce. After eight years of war with England, he finally became the undisputed King of Scotland. It is said that when in hiding, he found the courage to fight on from watching a spider trying again and again to climb its web.**

THE HUNDRED YEARS WAR BEGINS

The Hundred Years War between England and France was a series of wars, interspersed with truces. Edward III started the war in 1337, when Charles IV of France died without a direct heir. Edward wanted to secure his claim to the French throne through his mother, Isabella of France. Philip of Valois, who took the French throne, was anxious to regain Gascony, the last major English territory in France. Edward was spurred on by the ideas of chivalry and honour and also knew that if he could unite his restless barons in an overseas quest for honour they were less likely to start trouble at home.

- **1269** Prince Edward goes on crusade. First toll roads in England

- **1272** Henry III dies: Edward I, though absent, proclaimed king (to 1307)

- **1274** Edward I arrives in England and is crowned king. Llewelyn the Last refuses to take oath of allegiance to Edward

- **1275** Edward holds his first Parliament. First Statute of Westminster; wool duties granted to the Crown

- **1277** Edward begins campaign in Wales against Llewelyn, who submits with Treaty of Conway

- **1282** Llewelyn's brother, David, begins a revolt against the English. Edward marches into Wales. Llewelyn killed in battle

- **1283** Welsh revolt collapses. David is executed. Edward begins building castles in Wales

- **1284** Statute of Wales, Welsh government organized

- **1291** Scots ask Edward to choose between 13 claimants to the Scottish throne

- **1292** Edward awards Scottish throne to John Balliol (to 1296), making Scotland a fief of England

- **1296** Edward invades Scotland (Balliol abdicates) and declares himself King of Scotland

- **1297** Wallace leads revolt in Scotland

- **1298** Edward defeats Wallace at Falkirk

- **1301** Edward makes his son, Edward, Prince of Wales

- **1305** Wallace executed

- **1306** Robert Bruce claims Scottish throne (to 1329)

- **1307** Death of Edward. Succeeded by son Edward II (to 1327). Bruce defeats English

Right: The Hundred Years War was not one long war but a series of short ones. It began in 1337 and ended in 1453 (actually 116 years). English longbowmen and pikemen fought French knights on horseback and crossbowmen. Knights who were given land in feudal times had to raise and equip an army if needed. Knights wore heavy armour and rode horses. Foot soldiers wore helmets and tunics.

FOCUS ON THE ORDER OF THE GARTER

Edward III founded the Order of the Garter in 1349 to carry on the medieval ideals of knighthood and chivalry. Legend has it that a countess accidentally dropped her garter while dancing with Edward III. The King picked it up and rebuked his sniggering courtiers with the quip *Honi soit qui mal y pense* (French for Warning be to him who thinks ill of this). This is now the motto of the Order. The garter is the highest order of knighthood.

EDWARD'S VICTORIES

Another cause of the Hundred Years War was the wool trade. The weavers of Flanders depended on English wool, and England's wool was their only source of income apart from farming. But the aristocratic rulers of Flanders were pro-French and attempted to curb the English wool trade. Edward III made a treaty with the Flemish weavers in 1338 to reinforce his claims against Philip VI who had already seized Gascony.

In the early years of the war the English won two major battles. The naval battle of Sluys in 1340 gave them control of the English Channel, and made an English invasion of France relatively easy. When the invasion began Edward had a major land victory at Crécy in 1346, on the banks of the Somme. This battle was won by Edward's longbowmen, whose arrows mowed down the French.

THE BLACK DEATH

During Edward III's reign, the greatest disaster befell Europe. In only twenty years the Black Death (bubonic plague carried by rats from Asia) killed about one third of Europe's population. The disease got its name from the spots of blood that formed under the skin and turned black.

The Black Death came to England in 1348, through Melcombe Regis, the port of Weymouth. Within a few weeks it had spread to London and Bristol, where at one stage the living were hardly able to bury the dead. Within a year almost every part of England and Wales had been affected. The death toll was half the country's population at that time.

- **1308** Edward II marries Isabella of France

- **1311** Privy Seal office is established

- **1314** Scots defeat English at the battle of Bannockburn

- **1320** Declaration of Arbroath: Scots lords state to the Pope their loyalty to Robert I (the Bruce)

- **1323** Edward and Robert agree truce

- **1324** French invade Gascony

- **1327** Edward deposed and; Edward III becomes king (to 1377). England regains Gascony

Below: Black rats on board merchant ships carried the bubonic plague in their blood and their fleas transmitted it to people.

Left: European streets in the Middle Ages were filthy places. Open sewers ran down the middle and there were rats and rubbish everywhere. Human waste was thrown out of windows with a cry of *"Gardez-loo"* to warn passers by to get out of the way. Disease spread because of dirt and rats.

● **1328** Edward III makes peace with Scotland. Philip VI becomes the first Valois King of France

● **1330** Edward arrests Roger Mortimer, Earl of March, and begins personal rule

● **1336** Trade with Flanders is halted. French attack Isle of Wight and Channel Islands

● **1337** Philip VI seizes Gascony: start of Hundred Years War. Edward claims French Crown

● **1338** French fleet sacks Portsmouth. Edward lands at Antwerp: makes alliance with German emperor. Flemish weavers make trade treaty with England

● **1340** English naval victory at Sluys wins control of English Channel. Parliament appoints auditors of the king's expenditure

● **1343** France and England make truce

● **1346** Edward defeats French at Crécy

● **1347** Edward captures French port of Calais

● **1348** Black Death reaches England. Edward founds the Order of the Garter

● **1350** Black Death reaches Scotland. Extension of Windsor Castle begins

● **1351** Statute of Labourers curbs wages

Below: **The effigy of the Black Prince that lies on top of his tomb in Canterbury Cathedral. He was a brilliant general. During the last years of his life illness made him bedridden and unable to control his armies.**

Many villages were abandoned because of the plague. One of these deserted villages has been reconstructed by archaeologists at Cosmeston, near Penarth in South Wales.

The Black Death also halted Edward III's campaign against Scotland, but Scottish rejoicing at this was soon dashed when the plague struck there too. Scotland, Ireland and Wales, however, suffered less severely than England. The Black Death lasted on and off for over 150 years.

THE BLACK PRINCE

Edward III's eldest son, Edward, Prince of Wales, was as fine a soldier as his father, and is known as the Black Prince because of the colour of his armour. In 1346 he distinguished himself by his bravery at the battle of Crécy when he was only 16. The French may have lost over 10,000 men against less than 200 English deaths. Here he won the three plumes and the motto *Ich dien* (German for I serve) used by princes of Wales ever since. A truce was made in 1348 but Philip VI died in 1350 and Edward attacked France again.

In 1356 Edward the Black Prince won his greatest victory as a commander at Poitiers, where he captured the French king, John II. This monarch was ransomed for 3 million gold crowns and the Duchy of Aquitaine. While fighting in Spain the Black Prince caught an infection which made him ill and he died in 1376, one year before his father.

Richard II

Above: Richard II (1377-1399) was a lover of art not of warfare and suffered from being unfairly compared with his father, the Black Prince, who was a great soldier.

Below: Richard II met with the rebels at Smithfield during the Peasants' Revolt in 1381.

When Richard succeeded Edward III he was only 10 years old and inherited the cost of the Hundred Years War which left the Crown deeply in debt. Richard II was too young to rule, so the country was governed for a decade by his uncles: John, Duke of Lancaster, generally known as John of Gaunt, and Thomas of Gloucester. Their rule was not popular and the introduction of heavy taxes led to the Peasants' Revolt in 1381.

LABOUR UNREST

The immediate effect of the Black Death had been a loss of a third of the labour force, and a rise in workers' wages which amounted to about 50 percent for craftworkers and agricultural workers, and 100 percent for women farm workers. Employers had little choice but to pay, but a Statute of Labourers in 1351 fixed the price of labour to be on the same scale as it had been before the Black Death. Labourers resented this law. The Statute was a failure.

- **1353** Edward III transfers the wool staple (market) from Bruges in Flanders to England

- **1356** Edward Balliol gives up throne of Scotland to Edward. Black Prince defeats and captures John II of France at Poitiers

- **1357** Treaty of Bordeaux between England and France

- **1360** France cedes Aquitaine, Ponthieu and Calais

- **1363** Statute of Apparel prevents people wearing dress above their station in life

- **1364** Hostage for payment of John II's ransom escapes: John returns to captivity, and dies

- **1366** Statutes of Kilkenny: Irish Parliament forbids the English overlords to marry the Irish and bans Irish language, laws and customs

- **1375** Peace with France: England left with only Calais, Brest, Bordeaux and Bayonne. Robin Hood appears in ballads

- **1376** The Good Parliament: first to elect a Speaker. Black Prince dies

- **1377** Edward dies: succeeded by 10-year-old Richard II (to 1399); regency council rules

- **1380** Wyclif translates Bible

- **1381** Peasants' Revolt

- **1387** Geoffrey Chaucer starts *The Canterbury Tales*

- **1388** Lords Appellant control government

- **1389** Richard II assumes rule

- **1393** Great Statute of Praemunire reasserts supremacy of State in Church affairs

- **1395** Irish chiefs submit to Richard

THE PEASANTS' REVOLT

The Peasants' Revolt of 1381 was led by Wat Tyler, a tiler (though some say a blacksmith), and Jack Straw (possibly a nickname). This open rebellion was sparked off by the imposition of a poll tax of one shilling per head.

More than 20,000 peasants from Kent and Essex marched on London. Here they killed the Archbishop of Canterbury who was also the Chancellor, whom they blamed for imposing the unfair taxes. They also burned John of Gaunt's palace, the Savoy. Richard II, still only 14 years old, faced a mob at Mile End and promised: "You shall have from me all you seek." Tyler and his men of Kent remained armed while the rest dispersed. A few days later, in the king's presence, Tyler was killed by the Lord Mayor of London, William Walworth.

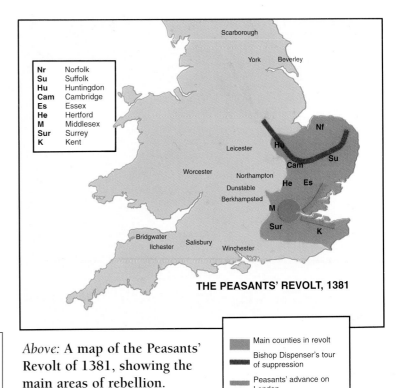

Nr	Norfolk
Su	Suffolk
Hu	Huntingdon
Cam	Cambridge
Es	Essex
He	Hertford
M	Middlesex
Sur	Surrey
K	Kent

THE PEASANTS' REVOLT, 1381

- Main counties in revolt
- Bishop Dispenser's tour of suppression
- Peasants' advance on London

Above: **A map of the Peasants' Revolt of 1381, showing the main areas of rebellion.**

FOCUS ON GEOFFREY CHAUCER

The poet Geoffrey Chaucer was born around 1340 and was squire to Edward III. He travelled to Italy on the king's business where he read books by Dante and Boccaccio. Chaucer wrote for Richard II's court, but his poems were read by a wider audience and were very popular. The most famous is a long poem called *The Canterbury Tales* which follows a group of pilgrims (some shown here) who tell each other stories on the way to Becket's shrine at Canterbury. It was the first important book written in English rather than Latin.

The Miller

The Prioress

The Knight

RICHARD II LOSES CONTROL

When the king's uncle John of Gaunt went off to Spain to pursue a claim to the throne of Castile, there was armed conflict between the king's men and the Duke of Gloucester who, in 1387, had set up a ruling council known as the Lords Appellant. In 1389, Richard took control of the government from the Duke of Gloucester, declaring "I am now old enough to manage my own affairs". For eight years the king's rule was peaceful and prosperous.

But when Richard's wife, Anne of Bohemia, died of the plague in 1394 he was left heartbroken and without purpose.

Richard turned into a tyrant, revenging himself in 1397 on the Lords Appellant. The Earl of Arundel was beheaded. The Duke of Gloucester, Richard's uncle, was murdered. Two others, Henry of Bolingbroke and the Duke of Norfolk, who had quarrelled, were banished. Soon afterwards John of Gaunt died, and Richard seized his estates. This was too much for John's son Henry of Bolingbroke. He returned from exile, swiftly gathered a large body of supporters, defeated the king's forces and took Richard prisoner to the Tower of London. By general consent Richard was deposed, and Henry succeeded to the throne as Henry IV in 1399.

Henry V (1413-1422) was a great soldier who won a famous victory over the French at Agincourt in 1415.

LANCASTER AND YORK
(1399 – 1485)

THE PLANTAGENETS were a fierce and quarrelsome family, and never more so than when disputing the right to the throne. Henry of Lancaster, son of John of Gaunt and grandson of Edward III, battled hard to become Henry IV, the first of the Lancastrian kings.

Much of Henry V's short reign was spent across the English Channel pursuing claims to France (England still held Calais and parts of Bordeaux) in the final stages of the Hundred Years War.

A complicated series of local civil wars involving various noble families who claimed the Crown marked the reign of Henry VI. A strong claim was put forward by Richard, Duke of York. The fighting that followed became known as the Wars of the Roses, from the red and white roses on the badges of the two conflicting families, Lancaster and York. In the end Henry Tudor, great-great-grandson of John of Gaunt, won the throne.

Scotland saw its throne pass to the Stewarts, a gallant and ill-fated family. Wales lost its independence and was gradually integrated with England, while the long struggle by the English to conquer Ireland continued.

Henry IV

HENRY IV had to struggle to hold the Crown, which he had seized by force. In 1400, a rising of Richard II's supporters was quickly crushed. Then Richard died in prison, probably murdered. But that was only the start of Henry's troubles. For the next five years, he had to face one rebellion after another.

Above: **Henry IV (1399-1413) was the first British king whose native language was English. He spent much of his reign fighting rebellions, as well as a major national uprising in Wales.**

THE LOLLARDS

In the late 1300s a religious movement had started in England which attacked many of the beliefs and practices of the Church of Rome. Its followers were known as Lollards, from a Flemish word meaning mutterer. They originally followed the teachings of John Wyclif, but later became more extreme. The Church saw them as heretics, and opponents of the established order of government.

To combat Lollardy, Henry IV's Parliament passed the cruel law *De Heretico Comburendo* (1401), which condemned heretics to suffer death by burning. Henry IV was the first English king to put men to death for their religious beliefs. Many followers of John Wyclif were burned at the stake.

OWEN GLENDOWER

Owen Glendower was the last independent Prince of Wales who ruled lands in North Wales. A feud with his neighbour, Lord Grey de Ruthyn, led to rebellion against England. Henry IV declared Glendower's lands forfeit, and gave them to Grey. Glendower raised an army and the Welsh backed him in what became, from 1402 to 1413 a national rebellion.

Right: **A breech-loading cannon of the 15th century. This cast bronze weapon fired solid balls which could knock down the thickest castle walls. Early cannons were not accurate and sometimes killed their loaders. The use of artillery (firearms) in battle and siege spread quickly throughout Europe. But English forces still relied on their longbowmen and knights on horseback to gain victory as at the battle of Agincourt in 1415.**

- **1399** Henry Bolingbroke seizes the throne as Henry IV

- **1400** Conspiracy by Earls of Huntingdon, Kent and Salisbury to kill Henry fails. Richard II dies in captivity. Henry campaigns in Scotland. Owen Glendower rebels in Wales

- **1401** Henry marries Joan of Navarre

- **1402** Henry enters Wales in pursuit of Glendower

- **1403** Revolt by the Percies: Henry kills Henry Percy (Hotspur) at Shrewsbury

- **1404** Glendower controls Wales, takes title Prince of Wales

- **1406** Prince James of Scotland captured by English on way to France. Robert III of Scotland dies; succeeded by captive James I (to 1420)

- **1409** Glendower's rebellion collapses

- **1410** St Andrew's University, Scotland, founded

- **1411** Henry, Prince of Wales, tries to control government. He is dismissed by Henry IV

Left: A 15th-century farmhouse. Yeomen or free farmers became increasingly prosperous in this period particularly if they had large flocks of sheep. Farmhouses like this one are still lived in today.

Below: Owen Glendower led Wales against England from 1400 to 1409. Defeated, but never captured, his final fate is unknown.

Henry IV was already troubled by uprisings in England, and Glendower had considerable success. For some years he virtually ruled Wales. But a successful campaign led by Henry's son, the future Henry V, broke the rebellion by 1409. Glendower's territory and castles were taken from him, but he evaded capture and disappeared.

THE CAPTIVE KING OF SCOTLAND

The Stewarts were in many ways an unlucky family. Most of the Stewart rulers came to the throne young, so the country was ruled by nobles in their name. Five of them died violent deaths.

Yet it was a Stewart, James VI of Scotland, who would unite the thrones of England and Scotland as James I of England in 1603, and the Stewarts (spelled Stuarts from then on) reigned until 1714. Queen Elizabeth II is herself descended from a daughter of James I of England (and James VI of Scotland).

The last years of the reign of Robert III of Scotland, in the early 1400s, were dominated by his brother the Duke of Albany, who was governor of the land. He was suspected of murdering Robert's heir, David. To safeguard his second son, James, Robert sent him to France by sea in 1406. English sailors captured the ship and James, who was 10 years old, was taken to London, where he remained a captive for 18 years, until 1424.

Robert went into deep mourning at the news of his son's capture, and died soon afterwards. The prisoner James was proclaimed King of Scotland. In captivity James wrote a long allegorical poem called *The Kingis Quair* (The King's Book). He also became a musician and an athlete.

FOCUS ON PILGRIMS

People of Christian faith in the Middle Ages went on pilgrimages for different reasons. Many went to seek forgiveness for their sins, or as a result of promises they made to God in return for His help. Others went seeking a miracle cure for an illness (just as people still go today to visit Lourdes in France). They visited famous shrines, monasteries and cathedrals around Britain, such as Becket's tomb at Canterbury. But many also travelled overseas, as far away as Jerusalem in the Holy Land.

The medieval pilgrim began his journey with a blessing by a priest, and on his return trip he would wear on his hat the badge of the shrine visited. The ones shown here are from Canterbury Cathedral. Along the way he would find hospices set up specially for pilgrims. Peasants, nuns, knights and merchants journeyed together. Pilgrimages were one of the few reasons many people had in the Middle Ages to travel long distances at home or overseas.

Henry V

DURING THE FINAL YEARS of Henry IV's reign much of the government passed to his son Henry, though the ailing king resisted any suggestion that he should abdicate. When Henry V came to the throne in 1413, he began by declaring a general pardon for his enemies and revived Edward III's old claim to the throne of France, which was occupied by Charles VI, who had suffered from fits of madness for the past 20 years.

The Dukes of Burgundy and Orleans were rivals for power in France. Henry allied himself with the Burgundians. The prospect of a war in France did much to unite the warring factions in England. Henry said to his father: "By your sword you won your crown, and by my sword I will keep it."

HENRY'S FRENCH CAMPAIGN

Henry's military campaign in France began by capturing the town of Harfleur at the mouth of the River Seine. From there he set out with about 5,000 men, 4,000 of them archers, to march east to Calais. The English found their way barred by a French army more than three times as strong. Attempts to negotiate a clear road to safety failed, and Henry resolved on battle. The French unwisely chose a narrow front between two woods, giving them no room to manoeuvre.

THE BATTLE OF AGINCOURT

Once again, against huge odds the English longbow won the day. This was the battle of Agincourt, fought on October 25, 1415; it was over in three hours, with the loss of almost 10,000 French dead and 2,000 captured, and only a few hundred English killed or wounded. Henry returned to England a hero. He had led the battle from the front, wearing his jewelled crown over his helmet. But Henry's army was too weak to attempt taking the French capital, Paris.

Right: The battle of Agincourt, 1415. A small English army defeated a much larger French one. The English strength was its archers, whose longbows showered the enemy with arrows. The wet weather also bogged the heavily armoured French knights in the mud.

Right: Henry V (1413-1422) is chiefly remembered for his victories against the French, including the battle of Agincourt in 1415. He was a chivalrous soldier and sensible ruler, but his gains in France were lost on his death.

DEATH OF HENRY V

Henry led a much larger expedition to France in 1417. Within three years he was master of Normandy. His ally, the Duke of Burgundy, was murdered by supporters of Charles VI's heir, the dauphin. This united the dauphin's opponents, who supported Henry V's claim to the French throne. Following the Treaty of Troyes in 1420, Henry was accepted as Regent of France, and as King Charles's heir. To cement the agreement Henry married the French King's daughter, Catherine of Valois. But two years later while on another campaign, Henry died of dysentery, a common disease among armies at that time.

Below: **It might take up to an hour for a knight to be fully dressed for battle. His esquire, or attendant, would strap or lace the leg armour on to the belt first, then came the breastplate and backplate and finally the gauntlets and the helmet.**

Left: **Full suit of plate armour**

Helmet

Joints in armour allowed some limb movement

Breastplate

A suit of plate armour could weigh 20 to 25 kg

Flexible chain mail underneath

Gauntlet

- **1413** Henry V becomes King of England (to 1422)

- **1415** Invasion of France: Henry captures Harfleur. Battle of Agincourt. Henry founds last monastery before Reformation at Twickenham

- **1417** Henry invades Normandy

- **1420** Treaty of Troyes: Henry to be Regent of France during life of Charles VI, and succeed him. Henry V marries Charles's daughter Catherine. Scottish Regent Albany dies; succeeded by son Murdoch (to 1425)

- **1422** Henry V dies suddenly; succeeded by infant son Henry VI (to 1461). Henry VI's uncles become regents: Humphrey of Gloucester in England; John of Bedford in France

- **1424** James I of Scotland is released, marries Joan Beaufort, and is crowned in Scotland

- **1428** James I calls for election of representatives of sheriffdoms to Scottish Parliament. English lay siege to Orleans in France; Joan of Arc hears "voices"

- **1429** Joan of Arc leads French to relieve city of Orleans. English defeated at Patay. Charles VII crowned King of France at Rheims

- **1430** Burgundian troops take Joan of Arc; hand her over to the English. Statute states shire-knights eligible for Parliament

Above: **A French archer loading a crossbow. The crossbow with its bolt, bowstring and stirrup (*see below right*) was powerful but much slower to load than the English longbow. English archers could fire 10 arrows a minute and their steel-tipped arrows could pierce armoured knights.**

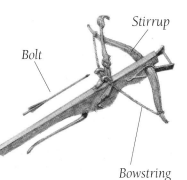

Stirrup

Bolt

Bowstring

Above: **Henry VI (1422-1461) went mad and had to submit his kingdom to a protector, Richard, Duke of York, from 1461 to 1470. He briefly claimed the throne again but was murdered in 1471.**

- **1431** Humphrey of Gloucester crushes Lollard uprising in Abingdon. Henry VI crowned King of France. Joan of Arc burned as a heretic in France

- **1433** Tattershall Castle, Lincolnshire, built with a million bricks

- **1436** Scots defeat English near Berwick

- **1437** Richard, Duke of York, captures Pontoise; Earl of Warwick becomes Regent of France. Murder of James I of Scotland: succeeded by son, James II, aged six (to 1460): Earl of Douglas is regent. Henry VI declared of age, but the Council of State holds power

- **1438** Truce between England and Scotland

- **1439** Congress of Calais: fruitless bid for Anglo-French peace. Henry Beaufort, great-uncle of Henry VI, controls the government. Regent Douglas dies. England makes truce with Burgundy

- *c.* **1440** Johannes Gutenberg invents printing from movable type

HENRY VI

Henry V left his English throne to his baby son, Henry, who was nine months old. Two months after becoming king of England, the baby Henry VI was proclaimed King of France on the death of his mad grandfather, Charles VI. His uncle, Humphrey Duke of Gloucester, was made regent in England. Another uncle, Duke John of Bedford, a skilled and experienced general, ruled France on his behalf. The French claimant to the throne, the dauphin Charles, controlled the country south of the River Loire, but England's hold on the northern region seemed secure.

JOAN OF ARC

In 1428 the demoralized French forces were given unexpected inspiration. Joan of Arc, a young peasant girl from Domrémy on the eastern border of France, heard voices and saw visions which commanded her to free her country from the English. One of the voices was that of the Archangel Michael, who appeared to her in a flood of light and told her to go to the help of the king. Joan went to the dauphin and said: "Gentle dauphin, I am sent to tell you that you shall be anointed and crowned in the town of Rheims, and you shall be lieutenant of the heavenly king who is the King of France".

During the siege of Orleans, Joan of Arc walked unseen through English lines one night during a storm and raised her banner from the battlements of the city to rally the French troops. Under her command the dauphin, Charles, marched to Rheims, where he was crowned King of France. Joan's voices then became silent, and she planned to return home. But she was captured by the Burgundian forces, who were still allied to England, and handed over to the English.

Above: **Map of France showing the main battles of the Hundred Years War, 1337–1453.**

Above: **Joan of Arc (1412-1431) was aged only 17 when she led the French to victory against the English at Orleans.**

Above: **Joan of Arc was tried and found guilty of heresy and sorcery by the Inquisition in 1431. She was burned at the stake by the English in the market place in the French city of Rouen.**

Left: **This was a period of great splendour in clothes for the rich. For men and women in the 1400s, an upper garment with long flowing lines was the most important piece of clothing: for men it could reach the knee, ankle or calf; for women it had long wide sleeves. Both men and women wore long hose, or stockings. For men these could be worn with leather soles attached, or with shoes or boots. Shoes had very long points. Turban-style hats were popular for men. Women favoured elaborate headwear.**

THE HUNDRED YEARS WAR ENDS

Joan of Arc was sold to the English who tried her for witchcraft and heresy, and burned her at the stake. An English soldier saw her die and said: "We are lost; we have burned a saint." In 1435 the valiant Duke of Bedford died, and in the same year the Burgundians finally broke their alliance with the English, and made a treaty with France.

Charles reorganized his army, learning from Joan's inspired victories that the once invincible English archers could be defeated by surprise attacks. Improved French artillery then pounded to ruins English fortresses. By 1453 the English had been almost completely driven out of France, and Henry VI had lost all his father's military conquests. The Hundred Years War was over.

HENRY VI: THE SCHOLAR KING

Henry VI's years as a child king saw bitter conflict between leading nobles competing for influence. When he came of age the situation had not improved; he was a gentle, pious and scholarly man, dominated by the powerful men around him.

When the Duke of Suffolk arranged Henry's marriage to the forceful French princess Margaret of Anjou, he signed a secret treaty ceding Maine to France. The English were furious when they found out. When the Hundred Years War ended in defeat for England, it was said that the Lancastrians, who had seized the throne by force, were unlucky for the country.

THE STRONG MAN OF SCOTLAND

James I of Scotland was released by the regents of Henry VI in 1424, after 18 years in captivity. He took back to Scotland an English bride, Joan Beaufort, granddaughter of John of Gaunt. But he found the land had been badly governed by his cousin Murdoch, son of the late regent, Albany. Within a year he had Murdoch and his sons executed. Within four years James had reorganized the Scottish government, strengthened Parliament, reformed the law courts and curbed the more rebellious of the Highland chiefs. Three of these chiefs he hanged; the rest he released after a short time in prison.

The Printing Revolution

THE CHINESE INVENTED a printing process using wooden blocks in the 6th century AD, and also produced a form of paper to print on. But printing by machines did not appear in Europe until the 1450s. By that time German-born Johannes Gutenberg had invented a printing press with separate pieces of metal type that could be moved around and could print individual letters. This printing method was slow, but the quality was the same for each copy and much easier to read than handwriting. For the first time many copies of a book could be made easily.

CAXTON AND THE FIRST BOOKS

The first book printed in English was produced in the 1470s by William Caxton. Before this, books were copied by hand in universities and monasteries, making them precious and rare. Only priests and nobles could afford to buy them.

William Caxton was born around 1422 in Kent, but moved to Bruges, in what is now Belgium, where for 30 years he was a rich merchant. At the age of 50 he moved to Cologne, in Germany, to learn the printing techniques of that country. In Bruges he set up his first press around 1474. There he produced the first book ever printed in English, a history of the legendary city of Troy, which he had translated himself.

In 1476 Caxton returned to England, encouraged by King Edward IV, and set up the first English press at Westminster, near London. With support from Richard III and Henry VII, Caxton later produced nearly 100 books, including Chaucer's *The Canterbury Tales* (in 1478). Many were printed in English rather than in the usual Latin and French, and some were his own translations of foreign books.

Above: A page from a book called *Legenda aurea*, printed by William Caxton at his press in Westminster. The picture is a woodcut of St Jerome. Before the first printing presses, there were only about 30,000 to 40,000 books in Britain. By the time of Caxton's death in 1491 there were over nine million.

Wooden block

Movable metal type

Above: **Block printing required a carver to cut the letters in reverse in one solid piece of wood, which could be used for only one job. Gutenberg introduced metal type which could be broken up and reused.**

Below: **In the Middle Ages books were not made of paper but of dried animal skins, on which scribes copied out text. The sheets were then stitched together by hand and bound between leather-covered boards.**

In Caxton's time there were often several different English words for one thing and many dialects, or regional variations, of English were spoken. Caxton chose one dialect for his books, and so helped establish a common language throughout the country. Caxton's type of printing press was used for 350 years, until the power-driven press.

HENRY VI AND PLANTAGENET FEUDS

While Henry VI was still a boy, the security of his throne came under threat from feuding uncles and cousins. Chief among them were the Beauforts, the descendants of John of Gaunt and his mistress, Katherine Swynford. The second Beaufort son, Henry, became Bishop of Winchester and was the richest man in the kingdom. Henry Beaufort competed for power with Humphrey, Duke of Gloucester, during Henry VI's minority, and influenced the feeble King when he came of age. These rivalries were to break out into what became known as the Wars of the Roses.

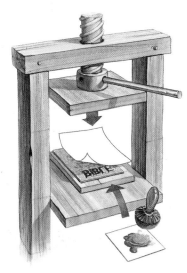

Above: **A printing press. The press was screwed down by hand and this squeezed the paper and type together. The invention of movable metal type meant that books could be produced** more quickly and efficiently. Printing was introduced into England by William Caxton in 1476. It helped to spread and establish a common English language instead of local dialects.

Left: **At first printing was carried out by rubbing an inked woodblock onto a sheet of paper. But Gutenberg invented movable metal type and adapted a wine press to apply pressure evenly over a whole sheet of paper. The ink was spread on a metal plate and then dabbed on the type with a leather-covered tool.**

Wars of the Roses

THE WARS OF THE ROSES were a series of conflicts for the English throne between families within the Plantagenet line. The main rivals were the House of York and the House of Lancaster, and these warring houses each had an emblem – the red rose of Lancaster, and the white rose of York – which gave its name to these wars.

The conflict between Lancaster and York was made worse by the barons, who were no longer fighting in France. Henry Beaufort's nephew John, Duke of Somerset, was the commander of Henry V's forces in France. After John's death, his brother Edmund, who became Duke of Somerset, led the English forces in the last battles of the Hundred Years War, and was a possible heir to the throne. Edmund's sister, Joan, married James I of Scotland. Several of the Beauforts died without children and others were killed in the Wars of the Roses.

Above: **The Wars of the Roses get their name from the badges of the two families involved: the red rose of Lancaster and the white rose of York. When Henry VII married Elizabeth of York he combined the two to form the Tudor rose (shown here).**

Right: **A map of England showing the movements and battles of the Yorkist and Lancastrian forces during the Wars of the Roses. The rivalry between the two great families ended with victory for Henry Tudor who was a Lancastrian.**

Below: **The crown of Edward IV, who became undisputed king during the Wars of the Roses after the battle of Tewkesbury in 1471.**

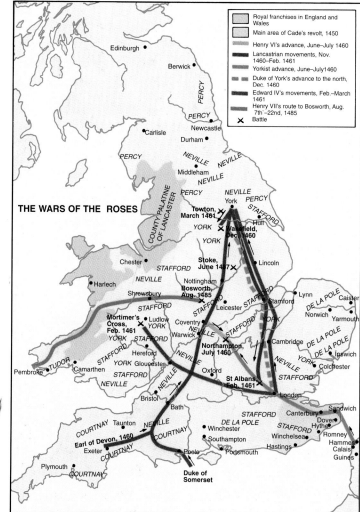

- **1440** English recapture Harfleur from the French. Douglas's sons murdered by order of councillors after dining with James II of Scotland

- **1441** Henry VI founds King's College, Cambridge

- **1444** William de la Pole, Duke of Suffolk, negotiates truce with France

- **1445** Henry VI marries Margaret of Anjou

- **1447** Parliament called at Bury St Edmunds, Suffolk. Humphrey of Gloucester arrested and dies in captivity

- **1449** English sack Fougères, Brittany: war with France resumes. Richard of York becomes Lord Lieutenant of Ireland; Edmund, Duke of Somerset, leads English in France

- **1450** Duke of Suffolk accused of selling the realm to France, and is murdered on way to exile. Jack Cade's Rebellion: 30,000 rebels from Kent and Sussex control London for a few days

- **1451** French capture Bordeaux and Bayonne, leaving England only Calais

- **1453** Henry VI becomes insane: York is regent

- **1454** Henry recovers; infant son Edward becomes Prince of Wales

- **1455** Wars of the Roses begin. Battle of St Albans: Yorkist victory. Henry VI captured. York becomes Lord Protector

- **1456** Queen Margaret dismisses York

- **1459** Civil war renewed: Lancastrian victory at battles of Bloreheath and Ludford

- **1460** Battle of Northampton: Yorkists capture Henry VI again. He agrees to York's succession

Above: **The Lancastrian King Henry VI at his Court as shown in an illuminated manuscript. In 1453 Henry suffered the first of several periods** of insanity. Richard, Duke of York became Protector because Henry was unable to carry out his duties as King of England.

Lord Protector. Somerset was blamed for defeats in France towards the end of the Hundred Years War, and was sent to the Tower. Almost as suddenly as he went mad, King Henry VI recovered. But Queen Margaret still controlled the king, and she now influenced the dismissal of York as Lord Protector and the release of Somerset.

York still did not openly claim the Crown, but he decided to fight against the hostile Margaret. His army met that of Margaret, Henry and Somerset at St Albans. Somerset was killed, Henry VI was captured and York briefly became Lord Protector again. After a few years of uneasy peace fighting broke out again and the Lancastrians won. York was killed.

WARWICK THE KINGMAKER

After the death of the Duke of York in 1460, the Yorkist leadership passed to his son, Edward, who was only 19 years old. One of the most powerful nobles, Edward's cousin Richard Neville, Earl of Warwick, became the power behind the throne during the Wars of the Roses. His intrigues gave him the nickname of the Kingmaker. Warwick Castle today provides a spectacular reminder of this turbulent period.

This left John's daughter, Margaret Beaufort, as the Lancastrian heir. She married Edmund Tudor, Earl of Richmond and was the mother of the future king, Henry VII.

YORK VERSUS LANCASTER

For some years after he married, Henry VI had no heir. There were two obvious candidates for the succession. Richard, Duke of York, was descended through his father from Edward III's youngest son, Edmund, and through his mother from Edward's second son, Lionel. He had a better claim to the throne than the king himself. The other candidate was the Lancastrian Edmund Beaufort, Duke of Somerset. Like Henry VI, Edmund was descended from Edward III's third son, John of Gaunt, but like all Beauforts he was barred from the throne. But he was still a favourite of King Henry and his queen, Margaret of Anjou. York, an honest and competent man, did not press his claim.

FIGHTING BEGINS

In 1453 King Henry went mad. During the same year his wife gave birth to a son, Edward. Law and order had almost completely broken down and unruly groups of soldiers, returned from fighting in France, roamed the countryside. York was made

Above: **Warwick Castle, the base for Richard Neville, an** important leader in the Wars of the Roses.

Left: Edward IV (1461-1483) was the first Yorkist king. He was a very tall, handsome and strong leader who brought a period of peace and prosperity to England. During his reign the arts also flourished.

Below: The battle of Bosworth Field in Leicestershire. Henry Tudor, who lived in exile in France, invaded England to claim the Crown by force. On August 22, 1485, Richard III was hacked to death by Henry Tudor's forces. In this picture, Henry kneels as he is crowned with a golden coronet. Legend says that the coronet was found on the battlefield from under a gorse bush.

- **1460** James II of Scotland killed by exploding cannon at Roxburgh: succeeded by James III, aged eight (to 1488)

- **1460** Battle of Wakefield: Lancastrian victory. Richard of York killed

- **1461** Battle of Mortimer's Cross: Richard's son, Edward, Duke of York, defeats Lancastrians. Second battle of St Albans: Margaret rescues Henry VI, defeats Earl of Warwick. York assumes the Crown as Edward IV (to 1483). Battle of Towton: Lancastrians defeated. Henry flees to Scotland

- **1462** Warwick crushes Lancastrians

- **1463** Edward again defeats Lancastrians: Margaret flees to France

- **1464** Edward crushes more Lancastrian rebellions. Yorkists capture Henry. Edward marries Elizabeth Woodville

- **1466** Lord Boyd kidnaps James III and becomes governor of Scotland

EDWARD OF YORK

In the 1460s the civil war became more intense with each side seeking vengeance for the killing of its own supporters. After several battles, Edward of York entered London and was proclaimed king as Edward IV. Soon afterwards, the battle of Towton crushed the Lancastrians. Despite this, the Lancastrian cause was kept alive by Queen Margaret, who still favoured Edmund Beaufort. Edward IV's marriage to Elizabeth Woodville brought her family to prominence and angered Warwick, who had hoped to arrange a French marriage for the king.

In 1469, Warwick rebelled and captured Edward. Warwick and Edward were reconciled but only briefly, and then Warwick had to flee to France. There, as a price for French help, he allied with his old enemy Queen Margaret. Warwick returned to England and won massive support; Edward in turn had to flee. Warwick restored King Henry VI to the throne, but his second reign lasted only a few months.

EDWARD'S VICTORY

Edward returned to England with troops from Burgundy. At the battle of Barnet (1471) Warwick was killed. At Tewkesbury, a few weeks later, the Lancastrians were finally crushed and many of the great barons killed. Henry VI's son Prince Edward was killed during the battle by Edward IV and his brothers. Yorkist Edward's battle cry had always been: "Kill the nobles and spare the commons!" Edward IV was then undisputed king. Henry VI was put back in the Tower and died shortly after, probably murdered.

EDWARD IV: FIRST YORKIST KING

Edward IV proved the strong and efficient ruler England badly needed. Popular demand called for the reconquest of the lost lands in France. He obtained funds through Parliament to finance an invasion but he also accepted money from the French not to invade, thus giving him two sources of income. He pursued a peaceful foreign policy which encouraged trade and kept taxes low. Also a ruthless king, Edward called another Parliament to condemn his treacherous brother George, Duke of Clarence, who died in the Tower.

EDWARD V: THE PRINCE IN THE TOWER

Edward IV had two young sons, and his rule and succession seemed secure. But at the age of 40 he was taken ill, and died within ten days. His 12-year-old son, Edward, succeeded him in 1483. But under the protectorship of his uncle, Richard, Duke of Gloucester, the reign of this young boy lasted just eleven weeks and one day.

Above: **Richard III (1483-1485) was the last Yorkist king. He was an energetic and competent king but made many enemies.**

- **1467** Scottish Parliament bans "fute-ball and golfe"

- **1469** Warwick changes sides, captures Edward IV, but lets him go

- **1470** Warwick forced to flee to France: he and Queen Margaret unite. Warwick lands with an army, restores Henry VI to the throne. Edward flees to Flanders

- **1471** Edward lands in Yorkshire with Flemish troops: resumes Crown. Battle of Barnet: Warwick killed. Battle of Tewkesbury: Prince of Wales killed. Margaret captured and Henry VI murdered in the Tower

- **1473** Edward sets up Council of the Marches to keep order in Wales

- **1475** William Caxton prints first book in English at Bruges. Edward plans to invade France, but is bought off by Louis XI

- **1476** Caxton prints first book in England at his press in Westminster. James III of Scotland subdues rebellion by John, Lord of the Isles

- **1483** Edward dies; succeeded by son Edward V, aged 12. Richard, Duke of Gloucester, is Regent: he declares Edward illegitimate and takes the throne as Richard III (to 1485). Edward and his younger brother disappear

- **1484** Heralds' College is founded. Richard III makes peace with Scots

- **1485** Henry Tudor, Earl of Richmond, invades England. Battle of Bosworth: Richard is killed and Wars of the Roses end. Henry Tudor takes throne as Henry VII

Right: A famous painting by Sir John Millais in the late 19th century. It shows the two young princes, 12-year-old Edward V and his 9-year-old brother Richard, who were sent to the Tower of London by their uncle Richard III and never seen again. Richard III was so loathed by his enemies that after his death at the battle of Bosworth, he was buried without ceremony and later his bones were thrown out and his coffin used as a horse trough.

RICHARD III

Richard, Duke of Gloucester, was renowned for his generalship, his abilities as an administrator, and his loyalty to the late king, Edward IV. Richard's strength was in the north but he was hated in the south. The Woodvilles, relatives of Edward's queen, Elizabeth, and Lord Hastings, one of Edward IV's generals, opposed his claim to the throne.

On Edward IV's death in 1483, Richard acted quickly: he accused Hastings of treason, and had him executed within the hour. Richard took Edward V and his young brother to the Tower "for safety"; they were never seen again. He told Parliament that Edward IV's marriage to Elizabeth Woodville (who also disputed Richard's claim) was invalid because Edward had previously made a marriage contract with someone else; the little princes were thus illegitimate. As a result, within three months of Edward IV's death, Parliament asked Richard to accept the Crown. At first Richard appeared to hesitate, but after some persuasion he accepted afterall.

The playwright William Shakespeare was later to portray the king as an evil hunchback in his play *Richard III*. But today many historians question whether he was so evil. In 1485 Henry Tudor, the last Lancastrian claimant to the throne, crossed from France and landed at Milford Haven in west Wales. He met Richard at the battle of Bosworth. Richard was deserted by many of his followers and killed. Henry Tudor was generally welcomed as Richard's successor and became Henry VII. The following year he married Edward IV's daughter, Elizabeth of York, thus ending the Wars of the Roses.

RULERS OF BRITAIN

HOUSE	NAME	REIGN	MARRIED	CHILDREN
PLANTAGENET	Henry II	1154 – 1189	Eleanor of Aquitaine	Henry the Young King, Richard I, Geoffrey, John
	Richard I the Lionheart	1189 – 1199	Berengaria of Navarre	
	John	1199 –1216	1. Hadwisa of Gloucester	
			2. Isabella of Angoulême	Henry III, Eleanor (married Simon de Montfort)
	Henry III	1216 – 1272	Eleanor of Provence	Edward I, Margaret (married Alexander III of Scotland), Edmund Crouchback
	Edward I the Lawgiver	1272 – 1307	1. Eleanor of Castile	Edward II
			2. Margaret of France	
	Edward II	1307 – 1327	Isabella of France	Edward III
	Edward III	1327 – 1377	Philippa of Hainault	Edward the Black Prince, Lionel, John of Gaunt, Edmund Duke of York
LANCASTER	Richard II (son of the Black Prince)	1377 – 1399	1. Anne of Bohemia	
			2. Isabella of France	
	Henry IV (son of John of Gaunt)	1399 – 1413	1. Mary de Bohun	Henry V, John Duke of Bedford, Humphrey Duke of Gloucester
			2. Joan of Navarre	
	Henry V	1413 – 1422	Catherine of Valois	Henry VI
	Henry VI	1422 – 1461	Margaret of Anjou	Edward
YORK	Edward IV (descended from Lionel)	1461 – 1483	Elizabeth Woodville	Edward V and Richard (Princes in the Tower), Elizabeth (married Henry VII)
	Edward V	1483		
	Richard III	1483 – 1485	Anne Neville	

GLOSSARY

canonize to formally declare a person a saint. Used by the Roman Catholic Church

cede to give up land to another person or country

crusades a series of wars fought by Christians against Muslims for control of the Holy Land (part of the Middle East). The First Crusade was in 1096, the last in 1291

dauphin title of the direct heir to the French throne

excommunicate to expel from the Church

feudal system (till 1400s) a system under which people held land in exchange for services to a noble

heresy a religious belief that is against the usual, accepted form of religion

homage a public acknowledgement of respect or honour to a lord or superior

Inquisition a search or enquiry by the Roman Catholic Church into heresy, sometimes involving the torture and execution of disbelievers

Justiciar chief officer of state, Lord Chief Justice

mandate a command from a superior, such as the Pope, ordering a person how to act

medieval of the Middle Ages

Muslims followers of Islam; those who worship Allah and follow the teachings of Mohammed

Parliament Britain's highest governing body, which had its beginnings in Middle Ages

pilgrimage a journey to a sacred shrine at home or abroad to give thanks or seek religious salvation

Plantagenet originally the nickname of Geoffrey of Anjou from the sprig of broom, *planta genista*, which he wore as a badge

regent person who rules while monarch is either too young (known as a minority), too ill or too far abroad to govern effectively at home

Wars of the Roses conflicts between Yorkists and Lancastrians for the English throne, 1455-1485.

INDEX

ACKNOWLEDGMENTS

The publisher would like to thank the following for supplying additional illustrations for this book:

Picture research: Alex Goldberg, Elaine Willis

page 3, medieval market, Mark Peppé; p7, Magna Carta, The Bridgeman Art Library; p18, Henry V, The Bridgeman Art Library; p20, Henry IV, Mark Peppé; p21, pilgrim badges, Mark Peppé; p29, Henry VI, e t archive; p29 Warwick Castle, Spectrum; p32, Princes in the Tower, The Bridgeman Art Library